KETO BREAD MACHINE

COOKBOOK

Easy Keto Bread Recipes for Effortless Baking

in Your Bread Maker

Jennifer Tate

TABLE OF CONTENTS

INTRODUCTION

What screams more to self-satisfaction than the smell of bread baking in your house? Nothing for me, personally! Honestly, it's glorious realizing that I can enjoy the foods I ate most of my life while still adhering to the regulations of the ketogenic lifestyle. The delicious and inviting aroma and the anticipation of adding your ingredients to the bread are more than anyone can handle.

My name is Jenny Tate, and my love for food, health, and living the best life that I possibly can inspire me daily to come up with better and brighter ideas to keep the creativity and joy in baking alive!

I started my love affair with cooking as a young girl and dove into the profession headfirst. As a professional chef for over 15 years, I have promoted my passion for wellness, nutrition, and the lifestyle improvement many seek, seeing deeper into their dissatisfaction with bland diets and expensive alternatives.

My expertise revolves around professional cooking and recipe creation for healthier meal plans. I have authored several cookbooks and nutritional guides that have helped many people worldwide.

And the world is changing fast. We have gone through all kinds of fads and diet schemes that leave people feeling empty and raw with resentment when they cannot get to their goal weight or even worse when their health dictates them to change their lifestyle and they can't handle the foods that are now put in front of them. Such a shame!

This is a small part of why I have stayed so close to my passion for baking, which always needs constant motivation and support. It needs new blood and techniques or threatens to become untouchable and monotonous.

After the pandemic hit, things changed even further. More time at home meant spending time in the kitchen (my favorite place) and around loved ones. Inspiration to cook more interesting and enjoyable meals alone or with the family has hiked up the need for new ideas and solutions to make better and healthier choices.

This quick and easy cookbook challenges you to try new things and adjust your mindset so you can eat with a smile. I will focus on the techniques needed for baking with your nifty bread machine. We will jump into what the keto lifestyle requires, how to apply these requirements to your bread recipe, and what tricks can be squeezed in to guarantee success when so many others fail.

So here we are! Ready to jump into the newest chapter of feeding your soul? Keto baking in your bread machine is brilliant, and with this book, I will help you discover the easy way around ingredients and no-fuss methods to perfect your bread every time!

THE KETO IDEAL

When we think of keto, we think of the three main conglomerates of the concept:

- high fat
- high protein
- low carbohydrates

The typical 4:1 weight ratio of fat to the combination of protein and carbs. Not the hardest thing to get your head around in theory, but in the practical sense, it can start looking a lot more complex when so many foods are off the menu and the numero uno being bread. It's terrifying if you must start removing all those sneaky pleasures of pizzas or toasted sandwiches. The carbs you are generally allowed are those in vegetables, fruits, and milk products that provide dietary fiber and vitamins A and C, essential to a healthy body.

The ketogenic diet was first implemented for those with serious health conditions like diabetes, epilepsy, arthritis, Alzheimer's disease, and cancer. The body would be used to combat the symptoms by receiving more certain macronutrients than others, tricking it into rebuilding itself and repairing the damage done to cells. Later it became more popular for weight loss, a cure for migraines, and has been shown to even alleviate symptoms of menopause.

Normally the body would use carbohydrates and turn them into glucose which is the easy way to obtain energy, but those sugars, pastries, and white breads simply allow for the insulin to store fatter and release a lot less energy regularly. Keto, on the other hand, does somewhat the opposite, where one consumes a larger amount of fats and proteins, which in turn convert into fatty acids and ketone bodies in the liver, and that allows the body to run purely on fats, keeping energy levels more stable and longer lasting throughout the day.

THE ART OF GRAIN-FREE BAKING

One thing we know for sure about the ketogenic lifestyle is that grains like wheat, oats, and rice are a no-go. And when we talk about making keto-friendly bread, that still needs to apply.

No bread machine will make you see the light at the end of the tunnel if you do not consider what alternatives can replace those grains and other sources of gluten. Many recipes include some gluten ingredient or replacement to allow the bread to have that familiar texture we all love. It is important to note that breads baked without gluten are lower in vitamin B, folic acids, and iron, so using alternatives that still give you the right nutritional value is super-duper important.

Baking with a bread machine is not necessarily the same as baking by hand with an oven, but it is just as fun. There are some cool brands out there, but look, you don't need anything fancy, and buying second-hand is also very convenient. They are easy to use if you understand the methods needed to insert all the ingredients and allow them to do their job. It might take a couple of tries, but once you have the basics down, you can pop out loaves that look and feel right.

THE WHY'S AND THE WHERE'S

Why should you use a bread machine when you could simply pop into your local store and buy one of those packaged keto bread brands? Easy choice, right? Wrong!

In the long term, it is a negative slope. The price for those premade keto bread brands found in the stores or websites is not comparable to the price for the raw ingredients used at home regularly. And the taste can alter dramatically when a little TLC is added in the process.

Regarding the price of ingredients, yes, it can shock the system when you see those numbers on the shelves for a single packet of this and a single portion (mainly due to the lack of competition and mass production). But do not despair, my dears! Online bulk shopping is the way to go! I have advocated using bulk buying for years, especially for those who cook and bake keto regularly. Websites like Amazon and Costco are brilliant with their bulk prices. Ingredients like flaxseed meal and oat fiber are well-priced. If stored correctly, these dry ingredients can last and last and keep you baking like a champion with your trusty bread machine for months.

People often ask me about their guilt in having bread in the house after sticking to the regime for so long. My response: guilt is like an evil little devil on your shoulder that rarely compliments you when you stay on track and follow the plan. But as soon as you deviate, well! It nags and nags, and before you know it, you are crying on the kitchen counter because YOU THINK you ever so slightly veered off track. That is not the way it should go down! We can maneuver around the wants we have by adjusting the choices we make.

Remember, the amounts one has are the key factors to all things, and the keto diet is one of the most rigorous when setting limits. One cannot simply 'tuck in;' there are rules too. That open sandwich (a single slice, usually around 2.5 g of carbs per slice) is perfectly fine as long as you stay within your 50 g daily carb intake. As simple as that.

THE STEPS FOR BREAD MACHINE BAKING

Some recipes will state, 'Just add all your wet ingredients into the bread pan and then dump your dry ingredients; after that, press a few buttons, and after four hours or so, voilà, the perfect keto bread!' No, please don't do this. I have been a stickler about the correct process methods for machine baking for some time now. I cannot state this with more vigor: place your ingredients into your bread pan like you are an artist, and this is your artwork!

There is a basic method, and the method works! Let's take a look at how it should be done step by step with a recipe that is not gluten-free but packed with important ingredients that keep the bread stable, fluffy, and most important low-carb (2.5 g per slice):

1. First, insert your warm water into the bread pan (1 cup / 240 ml).
2. Then add your lightly beaten eggs at room temperature (2 large).
3. Then add in your bowl of already sifted oat fiber meal (½ cup / 64 g) and vital wheat gluten (1¼ cups / 156 g).
4. Followed by your flaxseed meal (2/3 cup / 85 g).

These next steps require the artistry:

5. Add your soft butter AROUND THE EDGES of the pan (2 Tbsp.).
6. Add your salt and sweetener AROUND THE EDGES of the pan (2 Tbsp.).
7. Add your xanthan gum ALL OVER the pan (½ tsp).
8. Add your honey AROUND THE EDGES of the pan (1 tsp).
9. Add your active dry yeast in the indentation in the middle (1 Tbsp.).

Now take a teaspoon and use the back to indent a small hole in the middle of the dry ingredients (not all the way to the bottom of the pan to not touch the water).

10. Add your active dry yeast in the indentation in the middle (1 Tbsp.).

The next step is to carefully fix the bread pan into the machine (you must click it into place) and close the lid.

What I usually do is select the following settings on my machine:

- **Gluten-free setting** (this usually means that the cycles will run twice to make sure the ingredients are mixed properly, and the gluten development sets in)
- **Crust:** Medium
- **Cycle:** Twice (this will usually auto-set when selecting the gluten-free setting)
  Loaf size: 2 pounds (+- 907 g)

Note that setting choices can change if you prefer harder or softer bread. That will require you to try out different settings on each bake.

Now you press the start button, and off it goes for the next 3½ hours or so. Most machines have a little window in which you can watch your little bread baby take shape.

When baking, with these amounts of ingredients, you can usually reap around 14 slices for the whole week! Which is perfect if you are not the only one munching them each day.

BREAD MACHINE PROGRAMS

BASIC BREAD

This setting is also known as BASIC, STANDARD, or WHITE BREAD. This is the all-purpose setting you'll probably use most often. The cycle takes three to four hours, depending on your machine. You can use this cycle for country bread if you don't have a FRENCH BREAD program.

There is sometimes the further choice of QUICK or RAPID within this cycle.

SWEET BREAD

The SWEET BREAD cycle allows doughs with a higher fat and sugar content to rise more slowly. This cycle has a longer rise and a lower baking temperature, around 250⯑, since the crust of sweet bread will brown more quickly.

This cycle usually uses a beep to add extra ingredients, like chopped or glazed fruit or nuts.

VARIETY

This was a standard feature for the older machines. The VARIETY cycle runs as long as the BASIC cycle. In addition, it has a beep and displays a signal to "shape". So, you can remove the dough after the second rise, fill and form it by hand, and then return it to the baking pan for a final rise and baking. You could use this cycle for a cinnamon swirl or monkey bread.

DOUGH

This setting may also be known as the RISE or MANUAL cycle. This is the setting to use when you want to mix and raise dough in the machine, remove the dough, shape it by hand, and bake it in your oven. Doughs prepared in this setting are intended to be formed into traditional loaves or in special ways, such as cloverleaf dinner rolls, egg twists, pizza, croissants, and baked in the oven.

FRENCH BREAD

There is often a EUROPEAN, CRISP, or HOMEMADE setting for the same purpose. This cycle has become the new rage in bread machine baking. Use this setting for crusty country bread with no fat or sugar that needs longer rising times, giving the yeast a long time to work. Older national machines have this cycle lasting seven hours, which would bring a smile to the face of a traditional baker from France.

QUICK BREAD

This setting, also known as CAKE, is for non-yeast batters leavened with baking powder or soda, such as quick bread and loaf cakes. This cycle mixes the ingredients (although older machines require that the mixing be done by hand and the batter poured into the pan without the kneading blade installed) and bakes without any rise time. There is an option for further baking at one-minute intervals. This cycle works well with packaged commercial mixes for cornbread, quick bread, and pound cake.

When you are on the keto diet, you do not need bread. However, if you love it, our recipes can make your culinary experience full again.

TIPS AND TRICKS FOR BEST RESULTS

- **Measuring ingredients** as per the recipe is obviously important. This applies to any baking project, not just the keto method. The ratio of some complex ingredients, like the flaxseed meal and VWG, is tricky and needs to be followed precisely.

- **Temperature and time** are thankfully already prompted in the machine if a certain setting is used. Bread machines vary, so read the instruction manual for more info on each use. The time is also set accordingly but usually takes around 4 hours.

- **Remove the bread** after the baking is finished and once it has cooled sufficiently. The bread pan is turned upside down on a breadboard or cooling rack and gently tapped at the sides to allow it to slide out. Sometimes the mixing paddle will stay stuck in the bottom of the loaf, so then just gently use a butter knife, and release it.

- **Storage** means wrapping up the loaf in a couple paper towels (absorbing the moisture released during the week) and sealing it either in a container or zip-lock bag and into the fridge it goes! Do not pre-cut the slices and then store them; cut each slice as you go during the week, so the bread stays fresher for longer (around 7 days).

- **Flaxseed meal** can be bought very coarsely at certain suppliers. For better results, try to find a more finely ground product so that it can interact with the VWG and promote better gluten development. If it is a rather coarse brand, freeze the flaxseeds first (so that no extra heat is generated, and they don't go rancid) and grind them into a finer powder. The main reason for flops is precisely this issue: the interaction between the flaxseed mucilage and the VWG mineral starch must have an adequate ratio to contain the gases and give it that shape.

- **Storage of dry ingredients** correctly can make the process a lot easier. Ensure your flaxseeds and vital wheat gluten are stored in the fridge and removed an hour before baking so they may reach room temperature.

Fat and protein content is crucial when assessing what your macro needs are during the preparation stages of baking. Do you want more fiber and less saturated fat? Have a look at the net carbs and fat content. If there is too much protein in the bread, it can kick your body out of ketosis. This happens when there is no glucose in your body, and the body has no choice but to convert the extra protein into glucose. So, make sure to adjust your ingredients according to your needs.

KEY INGREDIENTS

Almond powder is a gluten-free flour made from almond nuts. It can easily be made at home, as all you need to do is grind some almonds — in a blender, coffee mill, or spice grinder.

However, you should follow some simple rules:

- *Use only dried or fresh almonds.*
- *Grind a small number of almonds at a time.*
- *Don't grind a portion for over thirty seconds.*
- *Slightly shake the blender or grinder as you go.*

Pour boiling water over the washed nuts several times; peel; simmer; and grind them in a blender, coffee mill, or spice grinder. Be careful not to overgrind, as the almonds will begin to excrete oil after a certain point, turning your flour into nut butter. Sift the powder produced and regrind any oversized particles. Such flour is very hygroscopic so it can absorb and retain moisture. Therefore, almond-based baked goods are less likely to stale and stay fresh longer.

Almonds are rich in vitamins B, E, and A and in potassium, calcium, iodine, phosphorus, iron, and beneficial Omega-3 fatty acids. And they don't lose these valuable properties after heating. Almond flour inherits all the health benefits of nuts and is often beneficial for debilitated patients, people with allergies, and athletes. Some of the most welcoming qualities of almond flour include its ability to reduce/soothe pain, stop seizures, and raise hemoglobin levels, but it's most praised for strengthening the heart and blood vessels. However, be careful of nut allergies do not harm your health!

You can never add too many nuts; almond flour can contribute to almost any meal's taste and nutritional value. Almonds' sweet and somewhat milky flavor will make any recipe more festive and distinct and goes great in any dough, nut cream, or sweets.

Coconut flour is also gluten-free. This hypoallergenic product is a truly precious gift from a tropical paradise for all gluten-free and low-carb eaters. Neither coconut flour nor almond flour will rise when you add yeast.

Advantages of Coconut Flour:
- *As coconuts are not grains, their flour does not cause problems associated with cereal proteins.*
- *Coconut flour contains more protein, fiber, and iron than wheat flour.*
- *The protein content in the coconut flour is comparable to or higher than in whole-grain wheat (and still without gluten-related problems!)*
- *And here comes a special bonus… coconuts contain a lauric fatty acid that is also present in breast milk and famous for its antiviral and antibacterial properties.*
- *Unlike coconut butter, cream, and milk, the flour produced from dried coconut flesh does not have distinctive exotic taste.*

Disadvantages of Coconut Flour:

- *It might get pricey. However, the product is still cheaper than when using almonds.*
- *The high fiber content in coconut flour can be useful for some but may create specific problems for others.*

Coconut flour is best suited for pancakes, pies, and muffins, i.e., those baked goods should be fluffy and crumbly.

Secrets of Cooking with Coconut Flour:

- Always sift the flour before using it.
- Mix dough more thoroughly than with usual flour.
- Watch the baking time; it's often less than similar cereal-based foods.
- Coconut flour is very good at retaining moisture, so your baking will be more delicate than your usual gluten-free flour and won't stale that fast.
- You can store ready-to-use coconut flour at room temperature in a tightly-closed container for up to six months.

We are often asked if one flour can be substituted for another. It can, and these are the proportions:

1 cup of almond flour = 1/3 cup of coconut flour

1/3 cup of coconut flour = 2/3 cup of almond flour + 1½ tablespoons of ground psyllium husk powder

Keep in mind that the proportions may vary according to specific flour manufacturers.

Nut and seed flour

These can vary depending on the type of bread you are going for (white or brown bread), and a few flours that haven't been spoken about enough are chia flour, cashew flour, and chickpea flour. They all have great applications to the recipe, but it is important to evaluate the carb content of each.

Psyllium husk powder

Using this soluble fiber comes into play for two main reasons: helping to hold the bread together and lowering blood sugar levels drastically. Perfect replacement for xanthan gum.

VWG (vital wheat gluten)

This is not flour but is very similar in form. The powdery ingredient contains an all-gluten and mineral starch base and is considered one of the best binding agents. This product allows you to increase the nutritional value of your bread and give it a better crumb consistency.

Active vs. instant dry yeast

There is some speculation about whether using active dry yeast is better than instant dry yeast. The difference lies in whether you prefer to proof your dough with active yeast or skip the proofing and use instant yeast instead. I prefer using the active version as it allows you to assess whether the yeast is still alive and fresh, giving the bread a chewy texture.

Oat fiber

This is not a whole grain. Oat fiber is the husk of the oat grain and holds a large amount of insoluble fiber deducted from net carbs. It is a key ingredient in keeping moisture regulation, texture, and shelf life, and for me, most importantly, it prevents bowel obstruction.

Inulin, resistant scratches, and protein isolates

When added to your recipe, these soluble fibers and supplements assist in many ways. Both as a probiotic and stabilizer in the dough, they can improve insulin sensitivity and help reduce appetite.

Butter

Without butter, the bread will come out too 'light' in texture and not give the proper sensation of filling the stomach after a single slice. Try to stick to raw butter if possible.

Flaxseed meal

This adjusts the fat content of the bread as well. This ingredient contains very high amounts of omega-3 fatty acids and increases the proofing time of your baking.

Salt

Try using more pink salt over regular table salt when baking keto. Remember, you want to add as many microminerals to your mixture as possible, and Himalayan salt is far more nutritious. This gives more taste and combats the sweetness added when using honey or other sweeteners.

Eggs

Some keto breads have that 'eggy' taste that people do not enjoy, and we can counter that by replacing one of the eggs with a substitute or adding a sweetener. Eggs give bread protein punch and binding effect.

Xanthan gum

This magical ingredient can be used to replace the gluten used in VWG. Some prefer to remove the gum if they already have a strong gluten product used in the mix, but I like adding it into my baking process along with VWG to enhance the loaf structure even further. You will see your bread rise and stay firm if one adds just the smallest amount.

Honey

Adding honey (preferably raw) to the bake is controversial. The amount of carbs in honey can put people off, but depending on the amount used, it can combat the 'eggy' taste of the bread and give the yeast some leverage when baking. Plus, it is packed with micronutrients!

THE SUBSTITUTES

The main substitutes for each ingredient will depend on your personal flavor. To use honey or to not use honey? To use xanthan gum or to not use xanthan gum? This all comes down to your final net carb count for the loaf. Here are some alternatives you can use when substituting ingredients:

Natural sweeteners like monk fruit, Allulose, and Stevia are awesome replacements for honey. The amount of honey used counteracts the yeast, so the final net carbs are usually lower, but I completely understand why you might want other options. One must be careful with other sweeteners on the market as they contain tons of artificial additives.

Replacing eggs in bread baking is not too complicated. For example, you could take baking soda, vinegar, or pure Greek yogurt, but most people replace it with a flaxseed meal or chia seeds.

Xanthan gum can be replaced with cornstarch, chia seeds, flaxseeds, or psyllium husk.

The beauty of these replacements is that they are probably already in your cupboard if you are fully involved in the ketogenic life, so alternating ingredients with different bakes can help you get a better idea of what you prefer and test new flavor combinations.

Basic Bread

Lunch Bread

Enjoy your meal! 맛있게드세요
Bon appétit! SMACZNEGO!
Guten Appetit! On *Hyvää ruokahalua*
BUEN PROVECHO! *egin!* **Bonan apetiton!**
Dobar tek! BUON APPETITO *Dobrou*
Gero apetito! God appetit! *chut'*

Yields: 1½ pounds / 12 slices

Cooking time: 3½ hours

Crust: Light

Program: Basic

INGREDIENTS

- ½ cup (85 g) ground flaxseed
- 6 Tbsp. (50 g) coconut flour
- 1 cup + 2 Tbsp. (140 g) vital wheat gluten
- ¾ cup (180 ml) warm water (90F /32C)
- 2 whole eggs, slightly beaten

- 1½ Tbsp. unsalted butter, softened
- 5 sachets (5 g) Splenda sweetener
- ½ tsp kosher salt
- 2¼ tsp. active dry yeast

STEPS TO MAKE IT

1. Prepare all the ingredients for your bread and gather your measuring tools (a cup, a spoon, and kitchen scales).
2. In a large bowl, thoroughly combine the dry ingredients.
3. Carefully measure the wet ingredients into the bread machine pan.
4. Add the dry ingredients on top.
5. Close the cover. Set your bread machine program to BASIC and choose the crust color LIGHT. Press START.
6. Wait until the program is complete.
7. When done, take the bucket out and let it cool for 5-10 minutes.
8. Shake the loaf from the pan and cool for 30 minutes on a cooling rack.
9. Slice, serve, and enjoy the taste of fragrant homemade keto bread.

NUTRITION INFO (Per Serving)

Calories 123; Net Carbs 3.2 g, Total Fat 6.4 g; Saturated Fat 3.6 g; Cholesterol 31 mg; Sodium 107 mg; Total Carbohydrate 7.2 g; Dietary Fiber 4 g; Total Sugars 0.5 g; Protein 9.6 g, Vitamin D 5 mcg, Calcium 6 mg, Iron 1 mg, Potassium 63 mg

Low-Carb Bread

Enjoy your meal! 맛있게드세요
Bon appétit! SMACZNEGO!
Guten Appetit! On *Hyvää ruokahalua*
BUEN PROVECHO! *egin!* **Bonan apetiton!**
Dobar tek! BUON APPETITO *Dobrou*
Gero apetito! God appetit! *chut'*

Yields: 1½ pounds / 12 slices

Cooking time: 3½ hours

Crust: Light

Program: Basic/White Bread/Low-

INGREDIENTS

- 3 cups low-carb flour mix, packed
- 3 tsp. vital wheat gluten
- 1 cup (250 ml / 8 oz.) lukewarm water (80 - 90F /32C)
- ¼ cup (1.15 oz., 30 g) extra virgin olive oil
- 1½ Tbsp. sugar (don't scream, see the explanation)
- 1½ tsp. active dry yeast

STEPS TO MAKE IT

1. Dissolve the yeast and sugar in the lukewarm water in the bread machine pan and let it bubble. This may take 8 to 10 minutes.
2. Don't freak out about the sugar. It is necessary for activating the yeast, and it will be completely absorbed. It will not impact the total carb count.
3. Prepare all the ingredients for your bread and gather your measuring tools (a cup, a spoon, and kitchen scales).
4. Carefully measure the wet ingredients in the pan.
5. In a medium-sized bowl, thoroughly combine the dry ingredients.
6. Pour the dry ingredients over the wet ones.
7. Close the cover. Set your bread machine program to BASIC and choose the crust color LIGHT. Press START.
8. Wait until the program is complete.
9. When done, take the bucket out and let it cool for 5-10 minutes.
10. Shake the loaf from the pan and cool for 30 minutes on a cooling rack.
11. Slice, serve, and enjoy the taste of fragrant homemade keto bread.

NUTRITION INFO (Per Serving)

Calories 82; Net Carbs 6.9 g, Total Fat 4.8 g; Saturated Fat 1.1 g; Cholesterol 0 mg; Sodium 9 mg; Total Carbohydrate 8.5 g; Dietary Fiber 1.6 g; Total Sugars 5.8 g; Protein 2.2 g, Vitamin D 0 mcg, Calcium 1 mg, Iron 0 mg, Potassium 37 mg

Breakfast Bread

Yields: 1 pound / 8 slices

Cooking time: 1 hour

Crust: Light

Program: Cake

INGREDIENTS

- 6 Tbsp. (50 g) coconut flour
- 8 whole eggs, beaten
- 1 cup (8 oz., 225 g) cream cheese, softened
- 4 Tbsp. (56 g) unsalted butter, softened
- ¼ tsp. ground cinnamon
- 1 tsp. keto baking powder
- ½ tsp. vanilla extract

STEPS TO MAKE IT

1. Prepare all the ingredients for your bread and gather your measuring tools (a cup, a spoon, and kitchen scales).

2. Carefully put the ingredients into the bread machine pan.

3. Close the cover.

4. Set your bread machine program to CAKE. The time may vary depending on your device. Press START.

5. Help the machine to knead the dough, if necessary.

6. After 40 minutes of baking, check for doneness using a toothpick. The approximate baking time is 40 - 45 minutes.

7. Wait until the program is complete.

8. When done, take the bucket out and let it cool for 5-10 minutes.

9. Shake the loaf from the pan and let it cool for 30 minutes on a cooling rack. Slice, serve, and enjoy the taste of fragrant keto bread.

NUTRITION INFO (Per Serving)

Calories 260; Net Carbs 3.6 g, Total Fat 21.5 g; Saturated Fat 12.7 g; Cholesterol 210 mg; Sodium 307 mg; Total Carbohydrate 7.4 g; Dietary Fiber 3.8 g; Total Sugars 1.2 g; Protein 9.2 g, Vitamin D 19 mcg, Calcium 59 mg, Iron 1 mg, Potassium 95 mg

Brunch Bread

Enjoy your meal! 맛있게 드세요
Bon appétit! SMACZNEGO!
Guten Appetit! On *Hyvää ruokahalua*
BUEN PROVECHO! *egin!* **Bonan apetiton!**
Dobar tek! **BUON APPETITO** *Dobrou chuť!*
Gero apetito! God appetit!

Yields: 1½ pounds / 12 slices

Cooking time: 3½ hours

Crust: Light

Program: Basic/White Bread

INGREDIENTS

- 1/4 cup (40 g) oat fiber
- 3/4 cup (100 g) organic soy flour
- 1/4 cup (40 g) flax meal
- 1/4 cup (25 g) coarse unprocessed wheat bran
- 1 cup (120 g) vital wheat gluten
- 1+1/8 cups (270 ml) warm water (90F/32C)

- 3 Tbsp. avocado oil
- 1 Tbsp. Splenda
- 1/2 tsp. sugar (see the explanation)
- 1 tsp. sea salt
- 1 pkg (2 tsp / 7 g) active dry yeast
- 1½ tsp. baking powder

STEPS TO MAKE IT

1. Dissolve the yeast and sugar in the lukewarm water in the bread machine pan and let it bubble. This may take 8 to 10 minutes.

2. Don't freak out about the sugar. It is necessary for activating the yeast, and it will be completely absorbed. It will not impact the total carb count.

3. Prepare all the ingredients for your bread and gather your measuring tools (a cup, a spoon, and kitchen scales).

4. Carefully measure the wet ingredients in the pan.

5. Pour the dry ingredients over the wet ones.

6. Close the cover. Set your bread machine program to BASIC and choose the crust color LIGHT. Press START.

7. Wait until the program is complete.

8. When done, take the bucket out and let it cool for 5-10 minutes.

9. Shake the loaf from the pan and cool for 30 minutes on a cooling rack.

10. Slice, serve, and enjoy the taste of fragrant homemade bread.

NUTRITION INFO (Per Serving)

Calories 86; Net Carbs 6.2 g, Total Fat 1.6 g; Saturated Fat 0.1 g; Cholesterol 0 mg; Sodium 153 mg; Total Carbohydrate 7.9 g; Dietary Fiber 1.7 g; Total Sugars 1.7 g; Protein 11.5 g, Vitamin D 0 mcg, Calcium 87 mg, Iron 1 mg, Potassium 327 mg

Almond Flour Bread

Enjoy your meal! 맛있게드세요
Bon appétit! SMACZNEGO!
Guten Appetit! On Hyvää ruokahalua
BUEN PROVECHO! egin! **Bonan apetiton!**
Dobar tek! BUON APPETITO Dobrou chuť
God appetit!

Yields: 1 pound / 8 slices

Cooking time: 3½ hours

Crust: Light

Program: Basic/White Bread

INGREDIENTS

- 2 cups (200 g) almond flour
- ¼ cup (36 g) Psyllium husk powder
- ½ cup (120 ml) warm water (90F /32C)
- 4 egg whites, whisked
- 4 egg yolks

- ¼ cup (60 g) unsalted butter/ghee, softened
- ½ tsp. sugar (don't scream, see the explanation)
- ½ tsp kosher salt
- 1½ tsp. active dry yeast

STEPS TO MAKE IT

1. Dissolve the yeast and sugar in the lukewarm water in the bread machine pan and let it bubble. This may take 8 to 10 minutes.
2. Don't freak out about the sugar. It is necessary for activating the yeast, and it will be completely absorbed. It will not impact the total carb count.
3. Prepare all the ingredients for your bread and gather your measuring tools (a cup, a spoon, and kitchen scales).
4. In a large bowl, thoroughly combine the dry ingredients.
5. Measure the wet ingredients into the mixture of dry ingredients.
6. Gently combine the mixture.
7. Pour the bread batter into the bread machine pan.
8. Close the cover. Set your bread machine program to BASIC and choose the crust color LIGHT. Press START.
9. Wait until the program is complete.
10. When done, take the bucket out and let it cool for 5-10 minutes.
11. Shake the loaf from the pan and cool for 30 minutes on a cooling rack.
12. Slice, serve, and enjoy the taste of fragrant homemade keto bread. Also, you can store it in the fridge or freeze it.

NUTRITION INFO (Per Serving)

Calories 116; Net Carbs 1.8 g, Total Fat 9.8 g; Saturated Fat 2.4 g; Cholesterol 43 mg; Sodium 14 mg; Total Carbohydrate 4.8 g; Dietary Fiber 3 g; Total Sugars 0.6 g; Protein 4.1 g, Vitamin D 3 mcg, Calcium 93 mg, Iron 1 mg, Potassium 20 mg

Snack Bread

Enjoy your meal! 맛있게 드세요
Bon appétit! SMACZNEGO!
Guten Appetit! On *Hyvää ruokahalua*
BUEN PROVECHO! *egin!* **Bonan apetiton!**
Dobar tek! BUON APPETITO *Dobrou chut'*
Geno apetito! God appetit!

Yields: 1½ pounds / 12 slices

Cooking time: 3½ hours

Crust: Light

Program: Basic/White Bread

INGREDIENTS

- 2/3 cup (64 g) almond flour
- ½ cup (56 g) coconut flour
- ¼ tsp. xanthan gum
- 1¼ cups (150 g) vital wheat gluten
- 1 cup (240 ml) warm almond milk (90F /32C)

2 Tbsp. ghee/unsalted butter, melted

2 tsp. liquid honey (see the explanation)

2 whole eggs (room temperature), slightly beaten

1 tsp. kosher salt

1 Tbsp. active dry yeast

STEPS TO MAKE IT

1. Dissolve the yeast and honey in the lukewarm almond milk in the bread machine pan and let it bubble. This may take 8 to 10 minutes.
2. Don't freak out about the honey. It is necessary for activating the yeast, and it will be completely absorbed. It will not impact the total carb count.
3. Prepare all the ingredients for your bread and gather your measuring tools (a cup, a spoon, and kitchen scales).
4. Carefully measure the wet ingredients in the pan.
5. Pour the dry ingredients over the wet ones.
6. Close the lid. Set your bread machine program to BASIC and choose the crust color LIGHT. Press START.
7. Wait until the program is complete.
8. When done, take the bucket out and let it cool for 5-10 minutes.
9. Shake the loaf from the pan and cool for 30 minutes on a cooling rack.
10. Slice, serve, and enjoy the taste of fragrant homemade bread.

NUTRITION INFO (Per Serving)

Calories 116; Net Carbs 4.5 g, Total Fat 4.8 g; Saturated Fat 1.4 g; Cholesterol 25 mg; Sodium 133 mg; Total Carbohydrate 5.4 g; Dietary Fiber 0.9 g; Total Sugars 1 g; Protein 13.5 g, Vitamin D 2 mcg, Calcium 14 mg, Iron 0 mg, Potassium 23 mg

Fiber Bread

Enjoy your meal! 맛있게드세요
Bon appétit! SMACZNEGO!
Guten Appetit! On Hyvää ruokahalua
BUEN PROVECHO! egin! **Bonan apetiton!**
Dobar tek! BUON APPETITO Dobrou
Gero apetito! God appetit! chut'

Yields: 1½ pounds / 12 slices

Cooking time: 3½ hours

Crust: Light

Program: Basic/White Bread

INGREDIENTS

- 2/3 cup (100 g) flaxseed meal
- 1¼ cups (150 g) vital wheat gluten
- ½ cup oat fiber
- ½ tsp. xanthan gum
- 1 cup (240 ml) lukewarm water (80 - 90F /32C)
- 2 whole eggs, slightly beaten
- 2 Tbsp. butter, softened
- ¼ cup (55 g) Xylitol
- 1 tsp. liquid honey (see the explanation)
- 1 tsp. sea salt
- 1 Tbsp. active dry yeast

STEPS TO MAKE IT

1. Dissolve the yeast and sugar in the lukewarm water in the bread machine pan and let it bubble. This may take 8 to 10 minutes.

2. Don't freak out about the honey. It is necessary for activating the yeast, and it will be completely absorbed. It will not impact the total carb count.

3. Prepare all the ingredients for your bread and gather your measuring tools (a cup, a spoon, and kitchen scales).

4. Carefully measure the wet ingredients in the pan.

5. In a medium-sized bowl, thoroughly combine the dry ingredients.

6. Pour the dry ingredients over the wet ones.

7. Close the lid. Set your bread machine program to BASIC and choose the crust color LIGHT. Press START.

8. Wait until the program is complete.

9. When done, take the bucket out and let it cool for 5-10 minutes.

10. Shake the loaf from the pan and cool for 30 minutes on a cooling rack.

11. Slice, serve, and enjoy the taste of fragrant homemade keto bread.

NUTRITION INFO (Per Serving)

Calories 58, Net Carbs 1.9 g, Total Fat 3.2 g; Saturated Fat 1.1 g; Cholesterol 22 mg; Sodium 156 mg; Total Carbohydrate 3.6 g; Dietary Fiber 1.7 g; Total Sugars 0.5 g; Protein 3.5 g, Vitamin D 3 mcg, Calcium 10 mg, Iron 2 mg, Potassium 54 mg

Almond Egg Bread

Enjoy your meal! 맛있게드세요
Bon appétit! SMACZNEGO!
Guten Appetit! On *Hyvää ruokahalua*
BUEN PROVECHO! *egin!* **Bonan apetiton!**
Dobar tek! BUON APPETITO *Dobrou chut'*
Gero apetito! God appetit!

Yields: 1½ pounds / 12 slices

Cooking time: 1 hour

Crust: Light

Program: Cake/Quick Bread

INGREDIENTS

- 2 cups (200 g) almond flour
- ¼ cup (37 g) psyllium husk powder
- ½ cup (120 ml) warm water (90F /32C)
- 4 whole eggs, beaten
- ¼ cup (54 g, 60 ml) coconut oil, melted
- ½ tsp kosher salt
- 1 tsp. gluten-free baking powder

STEPS TO MAKE IT

1. Prepare all the ingredients for your bread and gather your measuring tools (a cup, a spoon, and kitchen scales).
2. In a large bowl, thoroughly combine the dry ingredients.
3. Carefully measure the wet ingredients into the mixture of dry ingredients. Blend the mixture well.
4. Pour the bread batter into the bread machine pan.
5. Close the cover. Set your bread machine program to CAKE for 1 hour. The time may differ for different bread machines (50 – 80 minutes). Press START.
6. Wait until the program is complete.
7. Carefully test the bread for doneness with a toothpick. The top should be hard and crusty.
8. When done, take the bucket out and let it cool for 5-10 minutes.
9. Shake the loaf from the pan and cool for 30 minutes on a cooling rack.
10. Slice, serve, and enjoy the taste of fragrant homemade keto bread. Also, you can store it in the fridge or freeze it.

NUTRITION INFO (Per Serving)

Calories 118; Net Carbs 1.7 g, Total Fat 10.2 g; Saturated Fat 3.4 g; Cholesterol 36 mg; Sodium 34 mg; Total Carbohydrate 4.6 g; Dietary Fiber 2.9 g; Total Sugars 0.5 g; Protein 3.9 g, Vitamin D 3 mcg, Calcium 111 mg, Iron 1 mg, Potassium 13 mg

Nut Bread

Enjoy your meal! 맛있게드세요
Bon appétit! SMACZNEGO!
Guten Appetit! On Hyvää ruokahalua
BUEN PROVECHO! egin! Bonan apetiton!
Dobar tek! BUON APPETITO Dobrou
Geró apetito! God appetit! chut'

Yields: 2 pounds / 16 slices

Cooking time: 3½ hours

Crust: Light

Program: Basic/White/Low-Carb

INGREDIENTS

- 2/3 cup (64 g) almond flour
- ½ cup oat fiber
- 1¼ cups (150 g) vital wheat gluten
- 2/3 cup (160 ml) warm water (90F /32C)
- 1/3 cup (80 g) high-fat Amish sour cream
- 2 whole eggs, slightly beaten
- ½ cup (60 g) macadamia nuts, unsalted and roasted
- 2 Tbsp. unsalted butter, softened
- ½ tsp. xanthan gum
- 4 Tbsp. (160 g) Swerve
- 1 tsp. liquid honey (don't scream, see the explanation)
- 1 tsp. kosher salt
- 1 Tbsp. active dry yeast

STEPS TO MAKE IT

1. Prepare all the ingredients for your bread and gather your measuring tools (a cup, a spoon, and kitchen scales).
2. In a large bowl, thoroughly combine the dry ingredients.
3. Carefully measure the wet ingredients into the bread machine pan.
4. Add the dry ingredients on top.
5. Close the cover. Set your bread machine program to BASIC and choose the crust color LIGHT. Press START.
6. Wait until the program is complete.
7. When done, take the bucket out and let it cool for 5-10 minutes.
8. Shake the loaf from the pan and cool for 30 minutes on a cooling rack.
9. Slice, serve, and enjoy the taste of fragrant homemade keto bread.

NUTRITION INFO (Per Serving)

Calories 139; Net Carbs 8.2 g, Total Fat 11.3 g; Saturated Fat 3.1 g; Cholesterol 37 mg; Sodium 232 mg; Total Carbohydrate 10.1 g; Dietary Fiber 1.9 g; Total Sugars 6.5 g; Protein 6.1 g, Vitamin D 4 mcg, Calcium 40 mg, Iron 1 mg, Potassium 63 mg

Mediterranean Bread

Rosemary Bread

Yields: 1½ pounds / 12 slices

Cooking time: 1 hour

Crust: Light

Program: Cake

INGREDIENTS

- 2½ cups (240 g) almond flour
- 1 Tbsp. (15 g) coconut flour
- 2 Tbsp. unflavored protein isolate
- ½ cup (120 g) unsalted butter, softened
- 8 oz. (220 g) cream cheese, softened
- 8 whole eggs, beaten

- 1 tsp. dried rosemary
- 1 tsp. dried thyme
- 1 tsp. dried oregano
- 1 tsp. dried basil
- 2 Tbsp. garlic powder
- 1½ tsp. gluten-free baking powder

STEPS TO MAKE IT

1. Prepare all the ingredients for your bread and gather your measuring tools (a cup, a spoon, and kitchen scales).
2. Put all the ingredients into the bread machine pan.
3. Close the cover. Set your bread machine program to CAKE for 40 – 50 minutes and choose the crust color LIGHT. Press START.
4. Wait until the program is complete.
5. Check for doneness with a toothpick.
6. When done, take the bucket out and let it cool for 5-10 minutes.
7. Shake the loaf from the pan and cool for 30 minutes on a cooling rack.
8. Slice, serve with a piece of butter, and enjoy the taste of fragrant rosemary keto bread.

NUTRITION INFO (Per Serving)

Calories 288; Net Carbs 3.4 g, Total Fat 25 g; Saturated Fat 9.2 g; Cholesterol 128 mg; Sodium 240 mg; Total Carbohydrate 6.3 g; Dietary Fiber 2.9 g; Total Sugars 1.3 g; Protein 10.6 g, Vitamin D 13 mcg, Calcium 87 mg, Iron 2 mg, Potassium 54 mg

Zucchini Ciabatta

Yields: 4 servings

Cooking time: 30 minutes

Program: Dough

INGREDIENTS

- 1 lb. (4 cups, 450 g) zucchini, shredded
- 1 cup (112 g) almond flour
- 1 Tbsp. coconut flour
- 4 whole eggs, beaten
- ½ cup (70 g) sesame seeds

- 2 Tbsp. psyllium husk powder
- 1 Tbsp. Mediterranean herbs
- ½ tsp. kosher salt
- ½ tsp. coarse salt
- 1½ tsp. gluten-free baking powder

STEPS TO MAKE IT

1. Preheat oven to 400F (200C).
2. Prepare all the ingredients for your bread and gather your measuring tools (a cup, a spoon, and kitchen scales).
3. Put all the ingredients (except coarse salt) into the bread machine pan.
4. Close the cover. Set your bread machine program to DOUGH. Press START.
5. Wait until the program is complete. When the program is done, take the dough out.
6. Line a baking dish with parchment paper and spray it with olive oil.
7. Divide the dough into four equal parts. Place the dough portions on the baking dish. Sprinkle with coarse salt. Drizzle with olive oil.
8. Put the dish into a preheated oven and bake for 15 minutes or until golden brown.
9. Let it cool for 15 minutes on a cooling rack. Cut the ciabattas horizontally and serve with your favorite toppings.

NUTRITION INFO (Per Serving)

Calories 380; Net Carbs 10.4 g, Total Fat 28 g; Saturated Fat 4.1 g; Cholesterol 164 mg; Sodium 1435 mg; Total Carbohydrate 21.5 g; Dietary Fiber 11.1 g; Total Sugars 3.6 g; Protein 16.6 g, Vitamin C 15 mg, Calcium 501 mg, Iron 5 mg, Potassium 440 mg

Oregano Bread

Yields: 2 pounds / 16 slices

Cooking time: 3½ hours

Crust: Light

Program: Basic

INGREDIENTS

- 4 cups (450 g) low-carb bread mix
- ¾ cup (180 ml) warm water (90F /32C)
- ¾ cup (180 g) heavy cream
- 1 whole egg, beaten
- 2 Tbsp. canola oil

- 2 Tbsp. (27 g) Xylitol
- 1 Tbsp. dried oregano
- 1 Tbsp. dried rosemary
- 1½ Tbsp. active dry yeast

STEPS TO MAKE IT

1. Prepare all the ingredients for your bread and gather your measuring tools (a cup, a spoon, and kitchen scales).
2. Pour the wet ingredients into the bread machine pan.
3. Put the bread mixture, sweetener, and herbs on the wet ingredients.
4. Place the yeast in the center of the bread mix.
5. Close the cover. Set your bread machine program to BASIC and choose the crust color MEDIUM. Press START.
6. Wait until the program is complete.
7. When done, take the bucket out and let it cool for 5-10 minutes.
8. Shake the loaf from the pan and cool for 30 minutes on a cooling rack.
9. Slice, serve, and enjoy the taste of fragrant homemade keto bread.

NUTRITION INFO (Per Serving)

Calories 96; Net Carbs 4.4 g, Total Fat 4.8 g; Saturated Fat 2.2 g; Cholesterol 14 mg; Sodium 7 mg; Total Carbohydrate 10.7 g; Dietary Fiber 6.3 g; Total Sugars 0 g; Protein 3.5 g, Vitamin D 3 mcg, Calcium 12 mg, Iron 1 mg, Potassium 78 mg

French Bread

Yields: 1½ pounds / 12 slices

Cooking time: 3½ hours

Crust: Light

Program: Basic

INGREDIENTS

- 1 cup (112 g) almond flour
- ½ cup oat fiber
- 1 cup (120 g) vital wheat gluten
- 1 cup (240 ml) lukewarm water (90F /32C)
- 3 whole eggs (at room temperature), beaten
- 1/3 cup (76 g) butter, softened
- ½ tsp. xanthan gum
- 5 Tbsp. (40 g) erythritol
- 1 tsp. liquid honey (see the explanation)
- ½ tsp. kosher salt
- 1½ Tbsp. active dry yeast

STEPS TO MAKE IT

1. In the bread machine pan, dissolve the yeast in water with honey and let it bubble. It may be 8 - 10 minutes.
2. Don't freak out about the honey. It is necessary for activating the yeast, and it will be completely absorbed. It will not impact the total carb count.
3. Prepare all the ingredients for your bread and gather your measuring tools (a cup, a spoon, and kitchen scales).
4. Carefully measure the wet ingredients in the pan.
5. Pour the dry ingredients over the wet ones.
6. Close the cover. Set your bread machine program to BASIC and choose the crust color LIGHT. Press START. Wait until the program is complete.
7. When done, take the bucket out and let it cool for 5-10 minutes.
8. Shake the loaf from the pan and cool for 30 minutes on a cooling rack. Slice, serve, and enjoy the taste of tender French bread.

NUTRITION INFO (Per Serving)

Calories 143; Net Carbs 9.1 g, Total Fat 9.6 g; Saturated Fat 3.4 g; Cholesterol 47 mg; Sodium 61 mg; Total Carbohydrate 10.8 g; Dietary Fiber 1.7 g; Total Sugars 6.2 g; Protein 10.4 g, Vitamin D 6 mcg, Calcium 27 mg, Iron 1 mg, Potassium 40 mg

Italian Focaccia

Yields: 9 servings

Cooking time: 45 minutes

Program: Dough

INGREDIENTS

- 1½ cups (6 oz., 170 g) almond flour
- 1½ cups (200 g) mozzarella, melted
- 1 oz. (28 g) cream cheese, softened
- 1 whole egg, beaten
- 1 Tbsp. dried rosemary

- 2 Tbsp. olives
- Extra virgin olive oil spray
- ½ tsp. sea coarse salt
- 1 Tbsp. keto baking powder

STEPS TO MAKE IT

1. Preheat oven to 350F (176C).
2. Prepare all the ingredients for your bread and gather your measuring tools (a cup, a spoon, and kitchen scales).
3. Put all the ingredients (except the olives and salt) in a bread machine pan.
4. Close the cover. Set your bread machine program to DOUGH. Press START. Wait until the program is complete.
5. When the program is done, take the dough out.
6. Line a baking dish with parchment paper and spray it with olive oil.
7. Spread the dough evenly on the baking dish. Press the olives onto the top. Sprinkle with coarse salt. Drizzle with olive oil.
8. Put the focaccia into a preheated oven and bake for 15 minutes or until golden brown.
9. Let it cool for 15 minutes on a cooling rack. Slice, serve, and enjoy the taste of tender homemade focaccia.

NUTRITION INFO (Per Serving)

Calories 176; Net Carbs 3.1 g, Total Fat 14.1 g; Saturated Fat 3.4 g; Cholesterol 31 mg; Sodium 381 mg; Total Carbohydrate 5.3 g; Dietary Fiber 2.2 g; Total Sugars 0.7 g; Protein 9.8 g, Vitamin D 2 mcg, Calcium 89 mg, Iron 1 mg, Potassium 14 mg

French Baguette

Enjoy your meal! 맛있게 드세요
Bon appétit! SMACZNEGO!
Guten Appetit! On Hyvää ruokahalua
BUEN PROVECHO! *egin!* **Bonan apetiton!**
Dobar tek! **BUON APPETITO** *Dobrou chut*
God appetit!

Yields: 3 servings

Cooking time: 50 minutes

Program: Dough

INGREDIENTS

- 1/3 cup (30 g) almond flour
- ¼ cup (20 g, 0.7 oz.) psyllium husk powder
- 1/3 cup (30 g) coconut flour
- 1/3 cup (80 ml) lukewarm water (80 - 90F/32C⊠)
- ¼ cup (60 ml, 2.1 oz.) buttermilk
- 2 Tbsp. (30 ml) apple cider vinegar
- 3 egg whites
- 1 large egg
- 1 tsp. xanthan gum
- 1 tsp. kosher salt
- ½ tsp. baking soda

STEPS TO MAKE IT

1. Prepare all the ingredients for your bread and gather your measuring tools (a cup, a spoon, and kitchen scales).

2. Beat the eggs, egg whites, and buttermilk in a bowl.

3. Put all the ingredients in the bread machine pan.

4. Close the cover. Set your bread machine program to DOUGH. Press START. Wait until the program is complete.

5. Preheat the oven to 360F (180C).

6. When the program is done, take the dough out and shape it into a long roll. Make shallow cuts with a knife on the top of the baguette.

7. Place the baguette in the preheated oven and bake for 10 minutes.

8. Reduce the temperature to 320F (160C) and bake for 30-40 minutes.

9. Let it cool for 15 minutes on a cooling rack. Slice, serve, and enjoy the taste of a crispy homemade keto baguette.

NUTRITION INFO (Per Serving)

Calories 244; Net Carbs 10.6 g, Total Fat 8.4 g; Saturated Fat 1.3 g; Cholesterol 63 mg; Sodium 1038 mg; Total Carbohydrate 50.8 g; Dietary Fiber 40.2 g; Total Sugars 1.9 g; Protein 9.3 g, Vitamin D 6 mcg, Calcium 63 mg, Iron 1 mg, Potassium 84 mg

Olive Focaccia

Yields: 8 servings

Cooking time: 45 minutes

Program: Dough

INGREDIENTS

- ½ cup (60 g) coconut flour
- 5 Tbsp. (25 g) psyllium husk powder
- 1 cup (250 g) boiling water
- 4 large eggs, beaten
- 1 tsp. oregano

- 1 red onion, sliced into rings
- 2 Tbsp. black olives, sliced
- 1 tsp. coarse salt
- ½ tsp. kosher salt
- 1 Tbsp. gluten-free baking powder

STEPS TO MAKE IT

1. Preheat oven to 350F (176C).
2. Prepare all the ingredients for your bread and gather your measuring tools (a cup, a spoon, and kitchen scales).
3. Put all the ingredients (except onion, oregano, and salt) into the bread machine pan.
4. Close the cover. Set your bread machine program to DOUGH. Press START. Wait until the program is complete.
5. When the program is done, take the dough out.
6. Line a baking dish with parchment paper and spray it with olive oil.
7. Spread the dough evenly on the baking dish. Press the onion rings and sliced olives on the top. Sprinkle with coarse salt and oregano. Drizzle with olive oil.
8. Put the focaccia into a preheated oven and bake for 25 minutes or until golden brown.
9. Let it cool for 15 minutes on a cooling rack. Slice, serve, and enjoy the taste of savory homemade focaccia.

NUTRITION INFO (Per Serving)

Calories 66; Net Carbs 2.4 g, Total Fat 2.7 g; Saturated Fat 0.9 g; Cholesterol 93 mg; Sodium 448 mg; Total Carbohydrate 7.5 g; Dietary Fiber 5.1 g; Total Sugars 0.8 g; Protein 3.5 g, Vitamin C 9 mg, Calcium 218 mg, Iron 1 mg, Potassium 57 mg

Savory Bread

CAULIFLOWER BREAD	58
ZUCCHINI BREAD	60
BACON BREAD	62
TOMATO BREAD	64
GLAZED PUMPKIN BREAD	66
CHEESE KETO BREAD	68

Cauliflower Bread

Yields: 2 pounds/16 slices

Cooking time: 1¼ hours

Crust: Light

Program: Cake/Bake

INGREDIENTS

- 1¼ cups (140 g) almond flour
- 3 cups (600 g) cauliflower, cooked and mashed
- 6 egg whites, beaten
- 6 egg yolks
- 6 Tbsp. (80 g) avocado oil
- 1 tsp. kosher salt
- 1 Tbsp. keto baking powder

STEPS TO MAKE IT

1. Prepare all the ingredients for your bread and gather your measuring tools (a cup, a spoon, and kitchen scales).
2. Beat egg whites until peaks form.
3. Combine all the dry ingredients in a bowl.
4. Pour all the ingredients into the bread machine pan. Close the cover.
5. Set your bread machine program to CAKE for 60 – 70 minutes (depending on the bread machine model) and choose the crust color LIGHT. Press START.
6. Help the bread machine knead the dough with a spatula, if necessary.
7. After 35 minutes of baking, check for doneness using a toothpick. The approximate baking time is 40 - 55 minutes.
8. Wait until the program is complete.
9. When done, take the bucket out and let it cool for 5-10 minutes.
10. Shake the loaf from the pan and cool for 30 minutes on a cooling rack.
11. Slice, serve, and enjoy the taste of fragrant cauliflower keto bread.

NUTRITION INFO (Per Serving)

Calories 119; Net Carbs 2.7 g, Total Fat 9.1 g; Saturated Fat 1,4 g; Cholesterol 105 mg; Sodium 223 mg; Total Carbohydrate 4.9 g; Dietary Fiber 2.2 g; Total Sugars 1.2 g; Protein 6.2 g, Vitamin D 9 mcg, Calcium 63 mg, Iron 1 mg, Potassium 134 mg

Zucchini Bread

Yields: 2 pounds/16 slices

Cooking time: 1 hour

Crust: Light

Program: Cake/Bake/Quick

INGREDIENTS

- 2½ cups (285 g) almond flour
- 1 cup (110 g) zucchini, grated
- 3 large whole eggs, slightly beaten
- ½ cup (120 ml) extra virgin olive oil
- 1 tsp. vanilla extract
- 1½ cups (300 g) erythritol
- 1 tsp. cream of tartar

- ½ tsp. nutmeg
- 1 tsp. ground cinnamon
- ¼ teaspoon ground ginger
- ½ cup (75 g) walnuts, chopped
- ½ tsp kosher salt
- ½ tsp. baking soda

STEPS TO MAKE IT

1. Prepare all the ingredients for your bread and gather your measuring tools (a cup, a spoon, and kitchen scales).
2. Mix the cream of tartar with baking soda.
3. In a large bowl, thoroughly combine the dry ingredients.
4. In another bowl, blend the wet ingredients and add the zucchini to this bowl.
5. Put everything in the bread machine pan. Close the cover.
6. Set your bread machine program to CAKE for 60 – 70 minutes and choose the crust color LIGHT. Press START.
7. Before the BAKING mode begins, cover the top with walnuts.
8. Wait until the program is complete.
9. Check for doneness with a toothpick.
10. When done, take the bucket out and let it cool for 5-10 minutes.
11. Shake the loaf from the pan and cool for 30 minutes on a cooling rack.
12. Slice, serve with a piece of butter, and enjoy the taste of fragrant homemade keto bread.

NUTRITION INFO (Per Serving)

Calories 171; Net Carbs 3.9 g, Total Fat 16 g; Saturated Fat 1.8 g; Cholesterol 35 mg; Sodium 111 mg; Total Carbohydrate 6.2 g; Dietary Fiber 2.3 g; Total Sugars 2.3 g; Protein 6 g, Vitamin D 3 mcg, Calcium 46 mg, Iron 1.1 mg, Potassium 85 mg

Bacon Bread

Yields: 1½ pounds / 12 slices

Cooking time: 1 – 1½ hours

Crust: Light

Program: Cake/Bake

INGREDIENTS

- 1½ cups (170 g) almond flour
- 7 oz. (226 g) bacon, diced and fried
- 1/3 cup (80 g) sour cream, room temperature
- 1 cup (90 g) parmesan, grated
- 2 whole eggs, room temperature
- 4 Tbsp. (57 g) salted butter, melted
- 1 Tbsp. keto baking powder

STEPS TO MAKE IT

1. Prepare all the ingredients for your bread and gather your measuring tools (a cup, a spoon, and kitchen scales).
2. In a medium-sized bowl, combine all the dry ingredients.
3. Carefully whisk sour cream with eggs.
4. Pour all the ingredients into the bread machine pan. Close the cover.
5. Set your bread machine program to CAKE for 45 – 60 minutes (depending on the bread machine model) and choose the crust color LIGHT. Press START.
6. Help the bread machine knead the dough with a spatula, if necessary.
7. Before baking, sprinkle the top with grated cheese.
8. After 35 minutes of baking, check for doneness using a toothpick. The approximate baking time is 40 - 50 minutes.
9. Wait until the program is complete.
10. When done, take the bucket out and let it cool for 5-10 minutes.
11. Shake the loaf from the pan and cool for 30 minutes on a cooling rack.
12. Slice, serve with a piece of butter, and enjoy the taste of fragrant keto cheese bread.

NUTRITION INFO (Per Serving)

Calories 256; Net Carbs 2.6 g, Total Fat 21.6 g; Saturated Fat 7,4 g; Cholesterol 63 mg; Sodium 731 mg; Total Carbohydrate 4.1 g; Dietary Fiber 1.5 g; Total Sugars 0.6 g; Protein 12.8 g, Vitamin D 5 mcg, Calcium 148 mg, Iron 1 mg, Potassium 120 mg

Tomato Bread

Yields: 1 pound / 8 slices

Cooking time: ¾ hour

Crust: Light

Program: Cake/Bake

INGREDIENTS

- 1 cup (150 g) flaxseed meal
- 4 tsp. oat fiber
- 4 whole eggs
- 2 Tbsp. (30 g) salted butter, melted
- 1½ tsp. xanthan gum
- 2 Tbsp. sun-dried tomatoes, diced
- ¼ cup (22 g) parmesan, grated
- ½ tsp. dried basil
- ¼ tsp. garlic powder
- ¼ tsp kosher salt
- 2 tsp. keto baking powder

STEPS TO MAKE IT

1. Prepare all the ingredients for your bread and gather your measuring tools (a cup, a spoon, and kitchen scales).
2. Carefully whisk eggs and butter together.
3. Pour all the ingredients into the bread machine pan. Close the cover.
4. Set your bread machine program to CAKE for 30 – 45 minutes (depending on the bread machine model) and choose the crust color LIGHT. Press START.
5. Help the bread machine knead the dough with a spatula, if necessary.
6. Before the baking mode begins, sprinkle the top with grated parmesan.
7. After baking for 20 minutes, check for doneness with a toothpick.
8. Wait until the program is complete.
9. When done, take the bucket out and let it cool for 5-10 minutes.
10. Shake the loaf from the pan and cool for 30 minutes on a cooling rack.
11. Slice, serve with a soup or a salad, and enjoy the taste of fragrant homemade keto bread.

NUTRITION INFO (Per Serving)

Calories 88; Net Carbs 0.6 g, Total Fat 6.1 g; Saturated Fat 2.4 g; Cholesterol 48 mg; Sodium 243 mg; Total Carbohydrate 2.6 g; Dietary Fiber 2 g; Total Sugars 0.2 g; Protein 4.7 g, Vitamin D 5 mcg, Calcium 82 mg, Iron 2 mg, Potassium 81 mg

Glazed Pumpkin Bread

Yields: 1½ pounds / 12 slices

Cooking time: 1 – 1½ hours

Crust: Light

Program: Cake/Bake

INGREDIENTS

- 1+1/3 cups (128 g) almond flour
- ¼ cup (30 g) coconut flour
- ¼ cup (28 g) flaxseed meal
- 2 Tbsp. (20 g) psyllium husk powder
- 1 cup (220 g) pumpkin puree
- 4 whole eggs
- 1 Tbsp. keto baking powder
- 2 tsp. apple cider vinegar
- 1 Tbsp. pumpkin pie spices

- 5 Tbsp. (84 g) unsalted butter/ghee, softened
- 1 cup allulose
- ½ tsp. kosher salt

FOR THE GLAZE:
- 1 Tbsp. ginger, grated
- 1 Tbsp. water
- 6 Tbsp. (80 g) xylitol
- 1 pinch of kosher salt

STEPS TO MAKE IT

1. Prepare all the ingredients for your bread and gather your measuring tools (a cup, a spoon, and kitchen scales).

2. Combine all dry ingredients except the sweetener in a large bowl.

3. Carefully blend butter with the sweetener. Add eggs and vinegar.

4. Pour all the ingredients into the bread machine pan. Close the cover.

5. Set your bread machine program to CAKE for 60 – 80 minutes (depending on the bread machine model) and choose the crust color LIGHT. Press START.

6. Help the bread machine knead the dough with a spatula, if necessary.

7. After 40 minutes of baking, check for doneness using a toothpick. The approximate baking time is 55 - 70 minutes.

8. Wait until the program is complete.

9. When done, take the bucket out and let it cool for 5-10 minutes.

10. Combine all the ingredients for the glaze.

11. Shake the loaf from the pan and cool for 30 minutes on a cooling rack.

12. Spread the glaze on top of the bread.

13. Slice, serve, and enjoy the taste of fragrant pumpkin keto bread.

NUTRITION INFO (Per Serving)

Calories 177; Net Carbs 3 g, Total Fat 13 g; Saturated Fat 1 g; Cholesterol 69 mg; Sodium 174 mg; Total Carbohydrate 7 g; Dietary Fiber 4 g; Total Sugars 1 g; Protein 5 g, Vitamin C 0.7 mg, Calcium 48 mg, Iron 1.1 mg, Potassium 76 mg

Cheese Keto Bread

Yields: 1 pound / 12 slices

Cooking time: 1 – 1½ hours

Crust: Light

Program: Cake/Bake

INGREDIENTS

- 1½ cups (192 g) coconut flour
- 8 oz. (225 g) cream cheese, room temperature
- ½ cup (113 g) unsalted butter, softened
- ½ cup (120 g) sour cream, room temperature
- 8 whole eggs, room temperature

- ½ tsp. Italian herbs
- 1 Tbsp. allulose
- 1 tsp. kosher salt
- 2 Tbsp. sesame seeds, for garnish
- 4 tsp. keto baking powder

STEPS TO MAKE IT

1. Prepare all the ingredients for your bread and gather your measuring tools (a cup, a spoon, and kitchen scales).
2. Combine all dry ingredients except the sesame seeds in a large bowl.
3. Carefully blend cream cheese with butter until fluffy. Add eggs to the mixture and combine.
4. Pour all the ingredients into the bread machine pan. Close the cover.
5. Set your bread machine program to CAKE for 60 – 80 minutes (depending on the bread machine model) and choose the crust color LIGHT. Press START.
6. Help the bread machine knead the dough with a spatula, if necessary.
7. Before baking, brush the top with water and sprinkle with sesame seeds.
8. After 50 minutes of baking, start checking for doneness using a toothpick. The approximate baking time is 60 - 90 minutes.
9. Wait until the program is complete.
10. When done, take the bucket out and let it cool for 5-10 minutes.
11. Shake the loaf from the pan and cool for 30 minutes on a cooling rack.
12. Slice, serve, and enjoy the taste of fragrant keto bread.

NUTRITION INFO (Per Serving)

Calories 214; Net Carbs 3 g, Total Fat 20.2 g; Saturated Fat 11,4 g; Cholesterol 154 mg; Sodium 421 mg; Total Carbohydrate 3.8 g; Dietary Fiber 0.8 g; Total Sugars 0.4 g; Protein 6 g, Vitamin D 16 mcg, Calcium 85 mg, Iron 1 mg, Potassium 85 mg

Herb & Spicy Bread

SEED BREAD	72
HERB FLATBREAD	74
SEED BREAD	76
BASIL BREAD	78
GARLIC BREAD	80
SEADED BREAD	82

Seed Bread

Enjoy your meal! 맛있게 드세요
Bon appétit! SMACZNEGO!
Guten Appetit! On Hyvää ruokahalua
BUEN PROVECHO! egin! **Bonan apetiton!**
Dobar tek! BUON APPETITO Dobrou
Gero apetito! God appetit! chut'

Yields: 1 pound / 8 slices

Cooking time: 1 hour 10 minutes

Crust: Light

Program: Cake/Quick Bread

INGREDIENTS

- 2 cups (200 g) almond flour
- ¼ cup (36 g) Psyllium husk powder
- ½ cup (120 ml) warm water (90F /32C)
- 4 whole eggs (whites and yolks)
- ¼ cup (60 g) sesame oil
- 1 Tbsp. sesame seeds
- 1 Tbsp. sunflower seeds
- ½ tsp kosher salt
- 1 tsp. gluten-free baking powder

STEPS TO MAKE IT

1. Prepare all the ingredients for your bread and gather your measuring tools (a cup, a spoon, and kitchen scales).
2. In a large bowl, thoroughly combine the dry ingredients.
3. Separate the eggs into whites and yolks. Whisk the whites until peaks form.
4. Measure the wet ingredients into the mixture of dry ingredients.
5. Carefully combine the mixture.
6. Pour the bread batter into the bread machine pan. Close the cover.
7. Set your bread machine program to QUICK BREAD for 1 hour. The time may differ for different bread machines (50 – 80 minutes). Press START.
8. Wait until the program is complete.
9. Carefully test the bread for doneness with a toothpick. The top should be hard and crusty.
10. When done, take the bucket out and let it cool for 5-10 minutes.
11. Shake the loaf from the pan and cool for 30 minutes on a cooling rack.
12. Slice, serve, and enjoy the taste of fragrant homemade keto bread. Also, you can store it in the fridge or freeze it.

NUTRITION INFO (Per Serving)

Calories 123; Net Carbs 1.7 g, Total Fat 10.6 g; Saturated Fat 1.2 g; Cholesterol 36 mg; Sodium 85 mg; Total Carbohydrate 4.7 g; Dietary Fiber 3 g; Total Sugars 0.5 g; Protein 4 g, Vitamin D 3 mcg, Calcium 116 mg, Iron 1 mg, Potassium 17 mg

Herb Flatbread

Enjoy your meal! 맛있게드세요
Bon appétit! SMACZNEGO!
Guten Appetit! On Hyvää ruokahalua
BUEN PROVECHO! egin! Bonan apetiton!
Dobar tek! BUON APPETITO Dobrou chut'
Geno apetito! God appetit!

Yields: 1 tortilla

Cooking time: ½ hour

Program: Dough

INGREDIENTS

- ¼ cup (30 g) almond flour
- 1 cup (100 g) mozzarella cheese, shredded and melted
- 1 Tbsp. cream cheese
- 1 whole egg, slightly beaten
- 2 garlic cloves, minced

- ½ tsp. dried oregano
- ½ tsp. parsley
- 1 tsp. dried rosemary
- ¼ tsp. kosher salt
- ¼ tsp. black pepper

STEPS TO MAKE IT

1. Prepare all the ingredients for your bread and gather your measuring tools (a cup, a spoon, and kitchen scales).
2. Put all the ingredients into the bread machine pan.
3. Close the cover. Set your bread machine program to DOUGH. Press START.
4. Help the bread machine knead the dough with a spatula, if necessary.
5. Preheat the oven to 350F (180C).
6. Wait until the program is complete.
7. When done, transfer the dough to the baking sheet. Form flatbread.
8. Bake for 10-15 minutes or until golden brown.
9. Slice, serve with your favorite sauce or toppings, and enjoy the taste of fragrant keto flatbread.

NUTRITION INFO (Per Serving)

Calories 355; Net Carbs 7.1 g, Total Fat 27.2 g; Saturated Fat 7.7 g; Cholesterol 190 mg; Sodium 732 mg; Total Carbohydrate 11.2 g; Dietary Fiber 4.1 g; Total Sugars 1.5 g; Protein 20.9 g, Vitamin D 15 mcg, Calcium 153 mg, Iron 3 mg, Potassium 129 mg

Seed Bread

Enjoy your meal! 맛있게 드세요
Bon appétit! SMACZNEGO!
Guten Appetit! *On* *Hyvää ruokahalua*
BUEN PROVECHO! *egin!* **Bonan apetiton!**
Dobar tek! BUON APPETITO *Dobrou chut'*
Gero apetito! God appetit!

Yields: 1½ pounds / 12 slices
Cooking time: 35 minutes
Crust: Light
Program: Cake

INGREDIENTS

- 2½ cups (250 g) almond flour
- 2 cups (100 g) protein isolate
- 1 cup (240 ml) warm water (90F /32C)
- 1 Tbsp. xanthan gum
- 1 Tbsp. pumpkin seeds/sunflower seeds
- 1 Tbsp. hemp hearts
- 1 Tbsp. chia seeds
- 2 Tbsp. avocado oil
- ½ tsp. kosher salt
- 3 tsp. keto baking powder

STEPS TO MAKE IT

1. Prepare all the ingredients for your bread and gather your measuring tools (a cup, a spoon, and kitchen scales).
2. Add all the ingredients into the bread machine pan, following the instructions for your device.
3. Close the cover. Set your bread machine program to CAKE for 20 – 25 minutes. Press START.
4. Before the BAKING mode begins, sprinkle the seed mixture on the bread.
5. Check for doneness with a toothpick.
6. Wait until the program is complete.
7. When done, take the bucket out and let it cool for 5-10 minutes.
8. Shake the loaf from the pan and cool for 30 minutes on a cooling rack.
9. Slice, serve, and enjoy the taste of fragrant homemade keto bread.

NUTRITION INFO (Per Serving)

Calories 206; Net Carbs 3.2 g, Total Fat 13.9 g; Saturated Fat 1.1 g; Cholesterol 0 mg; Sodium 421 mg; Total Carbohydrate 7.6 g; Dietary Fiber 4.4 g; Total Sugars 0.9 g; Protein 17.3 g, Vitamin D 0 mcg, Calcium 112 mg, Iron 3 mg, Potassium 34 mg

Basil Bread

Yields: 1 pound / 8 slices

Cooking time: 1 hour 10 minutes

Crust: Light

Program: Cake/Quick Bread

INGREDIENTS

- 2 cups (200 g) almond flour
- ¼ cup (36 g) Psyllium husk powder
- ½ cup (120 ml) warm water (90F/32C)
- 4 whole eggs (whites and yolks)
- ¼ cup (60 g) extra virgin olive oil
- 1 Tbsp. olive tapenade (optional)

- 1 Tbsp. sage
- 1 Tbsp. dried basil
- 1 Tbsp. dried thyme
- 1 tsp kosher salt
- 1 tsp. gluten-free baking powder

STEPS TO MAKE IT

1. Prepare all the ingredients for your bread and gather your measuring tools (a cup, a spoon, and kitchen scales).

2. In a large bowl, thoroughly combine the dry ingredients.

3. Separate the eggs into whites and yolks. Whisk the whites until peaks form.

4. Measure the wet ingredients into the mixture of dry ingredients.

5. Carefully combine the mixture.

6. Pour the bread batter into the bread machine pan. Close the cover.

7. Set your bread machine program to QUICK BREAD for 1 hour. The time may differ for different bread machines (50 – 80 minutes). Press START.

8. Wait until the program is complete.

9. Carefully test the bread for doneness with a toothpick. The top should be hard and crusty.

10. When done, take the bucket out and let it cool for 5-10 minutes.

11. Shake the loaf from the pan and cool for 30 minutes on a cooling rack.

12. Slice, serve, and enjoy the taste of fragrant homemade keto bread. Also, you can store it in the fridge or freeze it.

NUTRITION INFO (Per Serving)

Calories 119; Net Carbs 1.9 g, Total Fat 10.2 g; Saturated Fat 1.2 g; Cholesterol 36 mg; Sodium 151 mg; Total Carbohydrate 5 g; Dietary Fiber 3.1 g; Total Sugars 0.5 g; Protein 4 g, Vitamin D 3 mcg, Calcium 119 mg, Iron 1 mg, Potassium 20 mg

Garlic Bread

Enjoy your meal! 맛있게 드세요
Bon appétit! SMACZNEGO!
Guten Appetit! On Hyvää ruokahalua
BUEN PROVECHO! egin! **Bonan apetiton!**
Dobar tek! BUON APPETITO *Dobrou chut'*
Gera apetito! God appetit!

Yields: 1 pound / 8 slices

Cooking time: 1 hour

Crust: Light

Program: Cake/Bake

INGREDIENTS

- 2 cups (8 oz., 200 g) almond flour
- ½ cup (2 oz., 60 g) mozzarella cheese, shredded
- 1 whole egg, beaten
- 1 tsp. garlic powder
- 1 tsp. kosher salt
- 1 Tbsp. keto baking powder

FOR THE TOPPING

- 1 Tbsp. unsalted butter, melted
- ¼ tsp. garlic powder
- ¼ tsp. kosher salt
- ¾ cup (3 oz., 90 g) mozzarella cheese, shredded
- ½ tsp. rosemary

STEPS TO MAKE IT

1. Prepare all the ingredients for your bread and gather your measuring tools (a cup, a spoon, and kitchen scales).

2. Put all the ingredients into the bread machine pan. Close the cover.

3. Set your bread machine program to CAKE for 30 minutes (depending on the bread machine model) and choose the crust color LIGHT. Press START.

4. Help the bread machine knead the dough with a spatula, if necessary.

5. After 10 minutes of baking, check for doneness using a toothpick. The approximate baking time is 10 - 15 minutes.

6. Mix the melted butter, salt, and garlic powder in a small bowl.

7. Five minutes before the baking process ends, brush the bread's top with the garlic butter, then sprinkle with the shredded mozzarella cheese and rosemary.

8. Wait until the program is complete.

9. When done, take the bucket out and let it cool for 5-10 minutes.

10. Shake the loaf from the pan and cool for 20 minutes on a cooling rack.

11. Slice, serve, and enjoy the taste of fragrant keto garlic bread.

NUTRITION INFO (Per Serving)

Calories 176; Net Carbs 3.7 g, Total Fat 14.9 g; Saturated Fat 1.4 g; Cholesterol 21 mg; Sodium 546 mg; Total Carbohydrate 6.7 g; Dietary Fiber 3 g; Total Sugars 1.1 g; Protein 7.3 g, Vitamin D 2 mcg, Calcium 95 mg, Iron 1 mg, Potassium 11 mg

Seeded Bread

Yields: 2 pounds/16 slices

Cooking time: 3 hours 10 minutes

Crust: MEDIUM

Program: Whole-Grain

INGREDIENTS

- 2 cups (200 g) almond flour
- 1½ cups (190 g) coconut flour
- ½ cup (120 ml) almond milk
- 1/3 cup (35 g) flax meal
- ¾ cup + 1 Tbsp. (190 ml) lukewarm water
- 2 tsp. tartar sauce
- ¼ cup (60 g) coconut oil, melted
- 3 whole eggs
- 1 Tbsp. maple syrup (don't scream, see the explanation)
- 4 Tbsp. (40 g) chia seeds
- 1 tsp. kosher salt
- 1 tsp. baking soda
- 2 tsp. bread machine yeast

STEPS TO MAKE IT

1. In a small bowl, combine the chia seeds and 1 teaspoon of flax meal with water and let it rest until it becomes a gel.
2. Whisk together coconut oil, maple syrup, eggs, and almond milk in a medium-sized bowl.
3. Don't freak out about maple syrup. It is necessary for activating the yeast, and it will be completely absorbed. It will not impact the total carb count.
4. Add the chia seed/flax meal gel to the medium-sized bowl and continue whisking.
5. Pour the wet mixture into the bread machine pan.
6. Put the remaining ingredients (except yeast) on top.
7. Place the yeast in the center of the bread mix.
8. Close the cover. Set your bread machine program to the WHOLE GRAIN and choose the crust color MEDIUM. Press START.
9. Wait until the program is complete.
10. When done, take the bucket out and let it cool for 5-10 minutes.
11. Shake the loaf from the pan and cool for 30 minutes on a cooling rack.
12. Slice, serve, and enjoy the taste of fragrant homemade keto bread.

NUTRITION INFO (Per Serving)

Calories 180; Net Carbs 3.5 g, Total Fat 15.6 g; Saturated Fat 5.7 g; Cholesterol 31 mg; Sodium 232 mg; Total Carbohydrate 7.6 g; Dietary Fiber 4.1 g; Total Sugars 1.8 g; Protein 5.7 g, Vitamin D 3 mcg, Calcium 62 mg, Iron 1 mg, Potassium 77 mg

Sweet Bread

"Banana" Bread

Enjoy your meal! 맛있게 드세요
Bon appétit! SMACZNEGO!
Guten Appetit! On Hyvää ruokahalua
BUEN PROVECHO! egin! Bonan apetiton!
Dobar tek! BUON APPETITO Dobrou
Geso apetito! God appetit! chut'

Yields: 1½ pounds / 12 slices

Cooking time: 1¼ hours

Program: Dough/Bake

INGREDIENTS

- 12½ cups (300 g) almond flour
- ¾ cup (180 g) sour cream
- 6 large organic eggs, beaten
- 4 Tbsp. (60 g) ghee, melted
- ½ cup (100 g) erythritol
- 1 Tbsp. banana extract
- 2 Tbsp. cinnamon
- ½ cup (60 g) walnuts, crushed
- ¼ tsp. ground nutmeg
- 1 Tbsp. keto baking powder

STEPS TO MAKE IT

1. Prepare all the ingredients for your bread and gather your measuring tools (a cup, a spoon, and kitchen scales).

2. In a large bowl, mix all the dry ingredients.

3. Beat the eggs with an electric mixer in a small bowl.

4. Pour eggs and wet ingredients into the bread machine pan.

5. Cover them with dry ingredients. Close the cover.

6. Set your bread machine program to DOUGH. The time may vary depending on your device. Press START.

7. Help the machine to knead the dough, if necessary.

8. After the program completes, start the BAKE mode for 55 minutes.

9. After 45 minutes of baking, check for doneness using a toothpick. The approximate baking time is 45 - 60 minutes.

10. Wait until the program is complete.

11. When done, take the bucket out and let it cool for 5-10 minutes.

12. Shake the loaf from the pan and let it cool for 30 minutes on a cooling rack.

13. Slice, serve, and enjoy the taste of fragrant "banana" keto bread.

NUTRITION INFO (Per Serving)

Calories 191; Total Fat 16.2 g; Saturated Fat 3.3 g; Cholesterol 78 mg; Sodium 173 mg; Total Carbohydrate 14.8 g; Dietary Fiber 2.9 g; Total Sugars 9.5 g; Protein 7.2 g, Vitamin C 7 mg, Calcium 74 mg, Iron 1 mg, Potassium 83 mg

Raspberry Bread

Enjoy your meal! 맛있게드세요
Bon appétit! SMACZNEGO!
Guten Appetit! On Hyvää ruokahalua
BUEN PROVECHO! egin! **Bonan apetiton!**
Dobar tek! BUON APPETITO Dobrou
Gene apetit! God appetit! chut

Yields: 1 pound / 8 slices
Cooking time: 1 hour
Program: Cake

INGREDIENTS

- 2 cups (200 g) almond flour
- 1 cup (100 g) raspberries
- 4 Tbsp. (60 g) sour cream
- 4 Tbsp. (60 g) unsalted butter, melted
- 2 whole eggs
- 1 tsp. vanilla
- 1 tsp. lemon extract
- ½ lemon (30 g), juiced
- ¼ cup (50 g) of your favorite sugar substitute
- 1½ tsp. keto baking powder

STEPS TO MAKE IT

1. Prepare all the ingredients for your bread and gather your measuring tools (a cup, a spoon, and kitchen scales).
2. Add all the ingredients (except the raspberries) to the bread machine pan, following the instructions for your device.
3. Close the cover. Set your bread machine program to CAKE for 40 – 50 minutes. Press START.
4. After the signal, add the raspberries to the dough.
5. Check for doneness with a toothpick. The approximate baking time is 45 minutes.
6. Wait until the program is complete.
7. When done, take the bucket out and let it cool for 5-10 minutes.
8. Shake the loaf from the pan and cool for 30 minutes on a cooling rack.
9. Slice, serve, and enjoy the taste of fragrant sweet keto bread.

NUTRITION INFO (Per Serving)

Calories 168; Net Carbs 8.3 g, Total Fat 14.8 g; Saturated Fat 3.8 g; Cholesterol 39 mg; Sodium 138 mg; Total Carbohydrate 11.1 g; Dietary Fiber 2.8 g; Total Sugars 6.3 g; Protein 5.3 g, Vitamin D 5 mcg, Calcium 64 mg, Iron 1 mg, Potassium 39 mg

Christmas Bread

Yields: 1 pound / 8 slices

Cooking time: ¾ hour

Program: Cake

INGREDIENTS

- ¾ cup (90 g, 3 oz.) coconut flour
- 4 large organic eggs
- ¼ cup (60 ml, 4 oz.) unsalted organic butter, melted
- 1 tsp. vanilla extract
- ¾ cup (150 g, 5 oz.) granulated Swerve

- 2 tsp. ground ginger
- 2 tsp. ground cinnamon
- ½ tsp. ground allspice
- ½ tsp. ground nutmeg
- ½ tsp. ground clove
- ¼ tsp. kosher salt
- 1 tsp. keto baking powder

FOR ICING

- ½ cup (120 g, 1 oz.) cream cheese, softened
- ¼ cup (40 g, 1 oz.) Swerve, powdered
- 1 tsp. vanilla extract
- ¼ cup (30 g) walnuts, chopped

STEPS TO MAKE IT

1. Prepare all the ingredients for your bread and gather your measuring tools (a cup, a spoon, and kitchen scales).

2. Whisk together the eggs, vanilla, and unsalted butter.

3. In a large bowl, mix all the dry ingredients.

4. Pour all the wet ingredients into the bread machine pan.

5. Cover them with dry ingredients. Close the cover.

6. Set your bread machine program to CAKE. The time may vary depending on your device. Press START.

7. Help the machine to knead the dough, if necessary.

8. After 30 minutes of baking, check for doneness using a toothpick. The approximate baking time is 40 - 45 minutes.

9. Wait until the program is complete.

10. When done, take the bucket out and let it cool for 5-10 minutes.

11. Shake the loaf from the pan and let it cool for 30 minutes on a cooling rack.

12. Slice, serve, and enjoy the taste of fragrant gingerbread cake.

NUTRITION INFO (Per Serving)

Calories 140; Net Carbs 13.3 g, Total Fat 12.9 g; Saturated Fat 6.5 g; Cholesterol 99 mg; Sodium 201 mg; Total Carbohydrate 14.3 g; Dietary Fiber 1 g; Total Sugars 12.3 g; Protein 4.4 g, Vitamin C 7 mg, Calcium 36 mg, Iron 1 mg, Potassium 67 mg

Berry Muffin Bread

Enjoy your meal! 맛있게 드세요
Bon appétit! SMACZNEGO!
Guten Appetit! *On* *Hyvää ruokahalua*
BUEN PROVECHO! *egin!* **Bonan apetiton!**
Dobar tek! **BUON APPETITO** *Dobrou chut'*
Geno spetito! God appetit!

Yields: 1 pound / 8 slices

Cooking time: 1 hour

Program: Cake

INGREDIENTS

- 2 cups (200 g) almond flour
- 4 Tbsp. (60 g) sour cream
- 4 Tbsp. (60 g) unsalted butter, melted
- ½ cup (50 g) blueberries
- 1/3 cup (67 g) of your favorite sugar substitute
- 2 whole eggs, beaten
- 1 tsp. vanilla
- 2 tsp. keto baking powder

STEPS TO MAKE IT

1. Prepare all the ingredients for your bread and gather your measuring tools (a cup, a spoon, and kitchen scales).
2. Pour the beaten eggs into the bread machine pan. Add all other ingredients.
3. Close the cover. Set your bread machine program to CAKE for 45 – 60 minutes (depending on your device). Press START.
4. After the signal indicating the beginning of the BAKE mode, add the blueberries.
5. After 35 minutes of baking, check for doneness using a toothpick. The approximate baking time is 45 - 50 minutes.
6. Wait until the program is complete.
7. When done, take the bucket out and let it cool for 5-10 minutes.
8. Shake the loaf from the pan and let it cool for 30 minutes on a cooling rack.
9. Slice, serve, and enjoy the taste of fragrant sweet keto bread.

NUTRITION INFO (Per Serving)

Calories 165; Net Carbs 9.8 g, Total Fat 14.8 g; Saturated Fat 3.8 g; Cholesterol 39 mg; Sodium 169 mg; Total Carbohydrate 12 g; Dietary Fiber 2.2 g; Total Sugars 8 g; Protein 5.1 g, Vitamin D 5 mcg, Calcium 63 mg, Iron 1 mg, Potassium 22 mg

Almond Sweet Bread

Yields: 2 pounds / 16 slices

Cooking time: 1 hour

Program: Cake

INGREDIENTS

- 2½ cups (250 g) almond flour
- 2 cups (140 g) whey isolate
- 1 cup (240 ml) lukewarm water
- ¼ cup (60 ml) almond milk
- ½ cup (100 g) powdered erythritol
- ½ cup (100 g) butter, melted
- 2 tsp. xanthan gum
- 1/2 tsp. kosher salt
- 1½ Tbsp. keto baking powder

FOR ICING:

- ½ cup (100 g) powdered erythritol
- 1 Tbsp. lemon juice
- 2 Tbsp. water

STEPS TO MAKE IT

1. Prepare all the ingredients for your bread and gather your measuring tools (a cup, a spoon, and kitchen scales).

2. Put all ingredients into the bread machine pan. Close the cover.

3. Set your bread machine program to CAKE. The time may vary depending on your device. Press START.

4. Help the machine to knead the dough, if necessary.

5. After 25 minutes of baking, check for doneness using a toothpick. The approximate baking time is 30 - 35 minutes.

6. Wait until the program is complete.

7. When done, take the bucket out and let it cool for 5 - 10 minutes.

8. Shake the loaf from the pan and let it cool for 30 minutes on a cooling rack.

9. Make the icing in a small bowl, mixing all the ingredients. Drizzle it over the bread.

10. Slice, serve, and enjoy the taste of fragrant sweet bread.

NUTRITION INFO (Per Serving)

Calories 130; Net Carbs 5 g, Total Fat 11.8 g; Saturated Fat 6.1 g; Cholesterol 21 mg; Sodium 248 mg; Total Carbohydrate 12 g; Dietary Fiber 1 g; Total Sugars 10.4 g; Protein 5.3 g, Vitamin C 5 mg, Calcium 60 mg, Iron 0 mg, Potassium 41 mg

Chocolate Bread

Yields: 1 pound / 8 slices

Cooking time: 1 hour

Program: Cake

INGREDIENTS

- ¾ cup (90 g) coconut flour
- 6 whole eggs, well-beaten
- ½ tsp. vanilla
- ½ tsp. Stevia
- 2 tsp. apple cider vinegar
- 4 oz. (1 stick/113 g) salted butter, melted
- 1 oz. (28 g) unsweetened baking chocolate, melted
- ½ cup your favorite keto sweetener

- ¼ cup (25 g) unsweetened cocoa powder
- ½ tsp. instant keto coffee
- ½ tsp. kosher salt
- ¼ tsp. xanthan gum
- 2 Tbsp. sugar-free chocolate chips (for garnish)
- 1 Tbsp. nuts, chopped (for garnish)
- 1 tsp. keto baking powder
- ½ tsp. baking soda

STEPS TO MAKE IT

1. Prepare all the ingredients for your bread and gather your measuring tools (a cup, a spoon, and kitchen scales).
2. In a large bowl, mix all the dry ingredients.
3. Beat the eggs with an electric mixer in a small bowl.
4. Pour eggs and wet ingredients into the bread machine pan.
5. Cover them with dry ingredients. Close the cover.
6. Set your bread machine program to CAKE for 60 minutes. The time may vary depending on your device. Press START.
7. Help the machine to knead the dough, if necessary.
8. After 40 minutes of baking, check for doneness using a toothpick. The approximate baking time is 45 - 55 minutes.
9. Wait until the program is complete.
10. When done, take the bucket out and let it cool for 5-10 minutes.
11. Shake the loaf from the pan and let it cool for 30 minutes on a cooling rack.
12. Garnish with chocolate chips and nuts.

NUTRITION INFO (Per Serving)

Calories 129; Net Carbs 12.1 g, Total Fat 12 g; Saturated Fat 6.9 g; Cholesterol 103 mg; Sodium 285 mg; Total Carbohydrate 13.5 g; Dietary Fiber 1.4 g; Total Sugars 11.3 g; Protein 3.8 g, Vitamin C 13 mg, Calcium 29 mg, Iron 1 mg, Potassium 86 mg

Sweet Keto Bread

Enjoy your meal! 맛있게드세요
Bon appétit! SMACZNEGO!
Guten Appetit! On Hyvää ruokahalua
BUEN PROVECHO! egin! Bonan apetiton!
Dobar tek! BUON APPETITO Dobrou chut'
Gesa apertol God appetit!

Yields: 2 pounds / 16 slices

Cooking time: 60 - 70 minutes

Program: Cake

INGREDIENTS

- 2 cups (200 g) almond flour
- 1 cup (130 g) coconut flour
- 4 avocados (400 g), mashed
- 1 cup (170 g) chocolate chips
- ½ cup (100 g) monk fruit sweetener

- 5 Tbsp. (70 g) avocado oil
- 4 Tbsp. (30 g) unsweetened cocoa powder
- 1 tsp. vanilla extract
- ½ tsp. kosher salt
- 1 tsp. baking soda

STEPS TO MAKE IT

1. Prepare all the ingredients for your bread and gather your measuring tools (a cup, a spoon, and kitchen scales).

2. In a large bowl, mix all the dry ingredients.

3. In a blender, combine all the wet ingredients.

4. Pour all the wet ingredients into the bread machine pan.

5. Cover them with dry ingredients. Add half of the chocolate chips.

6. Close the cover. Set your bread machine program to CAKE. The time may vary depending on your device. Press START.

7. Help the machine to knead the dough, if necessary.

8. Top the bread with the remaining ½ cup of chocolate chips before baking.

9. After 45 minutes of baking, check for doneness using a toothpick. The approximate baking time is 45 - 60 minutes.

10. Wait until the program is complete.

11. When done, take the bucket out and let it cool for 5-10 minutes.

12. Shake the loaf from the pan and let it cool for 30 minutes on a cooling rack.

13. Slice, serve, and enjoy the taste of fragrant chocolate avocado keto bread.

NUTRITION INFO (Per Serving)

Calories 290; Net Carbs 10.7 g, Total Fat 24.1 g; Saturated Fat 5.8 g; Cholesterol 3 mg; Sodium 187 mg; Total Carbohydrate 17.5 g; Dietary Fiber 6.8 g; Total Sugars 7.3 g; Protein 5.9 g, Vitamin C 0 mg, Calcium 66 mg, Iron 1 mg, Potassium 347 mg

Citrus Bread

Enjoy your meal! 맛있게 드세요
Bon appétit! SMACZNEGO!
Guten Appetit! On Hyvää ruokahalua
BUEN PROVECHO! egin! Bonan apetiton!
Dobar tek! BUON APPETITO Dobrou chuť
Good apetito! God appetit!

Yields: 1½ pounds / 12 slices

Cooking time: 1 hour

Program: Cake

INGREDIENTS

- 9½ oz. (270 g) almond flour
- 3 Tbsp. (60 g) unsalted butter, melted
- 6 whole eggs
- ½ cup (100 g) erythritol
- 2 Tbsp. poppy seeds
- 2 lemons zest
- 2 Tbsp. lemon juice
- ½ tsp. keto baking powder

FOR ICING:
- ½ cup (100 g) powdered erythritol
- 1 Tbsp. lemon juice
- 2 Tbsp. water

STEPS TO MAKE IT

1. Prepare all the ingredients for your bread and gather your measuring tools (a cup, a spoon, and kitchen scales).
2. Put all ingredients into the bread machine pan. Close the cover.
3. Set your bread machine program to CAKE. The time may vary depending on your device. Press START.
4. Help the machine to knead the dough, if necessary.
5. After 40 minutes of baking, check for doneness using a toothpick. The approximate baking time is 45 - 55 minutes.
6. Wait until the program is complete.
7. When done, take the bucket out and let it cool for 5 - 10 minutes.
8. Shake the loaf from the pan and let it cool for 30 minutes on a cooling rack.
9. Make the icing in a small bowl, mixing all the ingredients. Drizzle it over the bread.
10. Slice, serve, and enjoy the taste of fragrant lemon bread.

NUTRITION INFO (Per Serving)

Calories 193; Net Carbs 12.9 g, Total Fat 17 g; Saturated Fat 3.4 g; Cholesterol 89 mg; Sodium 85 mg; Total Carbohydrate 15.6 g; Dietary Fiber 2.7 g; Total Sugars 11.3 g; Protein 7.9 g, Vitamin C 10 mg, Calcium 87 mg, Iron 1 mg, Potassium 48 mg

FROM THE AUTHOR

Are you switching on that bread machine right this instant?
Are you so inspired by what you have just read that you are
off to the races exploding with a renewed vision for healthy
baking?

Well, if so, I am proud of you for choosing to go down this
road. It is a gift that keeps giving, and everyone around you
(including that little devil sitting on your shoulder) will thank
you. Now it is time for you to go and inspire your friends and
family and speak up about the keto bread revolution.

We have jumped from the keto ideal to the ideal bread
machine bake, and I hope with all my heart that each warm
and delicious loaf you make is filled with not only great-
tasting ingredients but plenty of love too.

I am positive that you have come out of this short but sweet
cookbook a brighter person. Eating better will return to you
tenfold later in life, so nourish your vessel and let the rest flow
easily.

OUR RECOMMENDATIONS

Keto Baking Cookbook: Easy Gluten-Free Recipes for Low-Carb Baking at Home. Everyday and Festive Pastry Ideas

Keto Bread Cookbook: Easy Keto Baking Recipes from Fragrant Bagels and Buns to Muffins and Breadsticks. Low-Carb and Gluten-Free Baking Recipes

Copyright

Made in the USA
Coppell, TX
04 December 2023

25360785R00059